GLASGOW TRAVEL GUIDE

2024

Discover the Charms Of Glasgow: A Comprehensive Travel Guide To Scotland's Vibrant City.

BY

Mia Aurora

Copyright

Table Of Contents

4

CHAPTER ONE

Introduction To Glasgow

Welcome to Glasgow, a dynamic and captivating city where modernity, culture, and history all coexist to provide a genuinely unforgettable travel experience. Glasgow, located in Scotland along the River Clyde, is a city bursting with personality and charm that offers a unique combination of architectural marvels, top-notch museums, exciting entertainment, and friendly Scottish hospitality.

A magnificent contrast of the old and the new will meet you as you travel through Glasgow's streets. In the skyline, sleek, modern buildings coexist with gothic and Victorian architecture, reflecting the city's rich history and commitment to innovation. Explore Glasgow Cathedral's architectural wonders, wander down Buchanan Street's bustling high-end stores, or take in the exquisite design of the Kelvingrove Art Gallery and Museum.

The cultural landscape of Glasgow is a diverse tapestry that appeals to all tastes. The expansive collection at the Burrell Collection will enchant art lovers, while live music fans may savor the city's bustling venues that have produced renowned performances throughout the years. While foodies may embark on a gastronomic trip by trying traditional Scottish foods and other cuisines at the city's numerous eateries, the historic Barras Market is a treasure trove for those looking for one-of-a-kind souvenirs, antiques, and vintage items.

Without learning about Glasgow's past and the legends that have influenced its culture, no trip there would be complete. The People's Palace provides insight into the life of the city's working-class residents, while the Riverside Museum offers an enthralling look into the city's industrial heritage. Don't pass up the chance to stroll through the mysterious lanes of the Merchant City neighborhood, where tales of trade, business, and craftsmanship are revealed around every corner.

To help you get the most out of your trip to Glasgow, we've thoughtfully produced this in-depth travel guide. Glasgow promises an extraordinary experience that will amaze and inspire you, whether you're an art fan, a history buff, a music enthusiast, or just looking for the warmth of Scottish hospitality. So, lace up your walking shoes, grab your camera, and get ready to set off on a journey through this fascinating city's heart and soul.

CHAPTER TWO

Welcome To Glasgow

2.1 Brief History Of The City

Scotland's Glasgow is a thriving, old-world metropolis with a fascinating history that dates back hundreds of years. Its transformation from a little town to a thriving city is evidence of its tenacity and enduring legacy.

Glasgow's founding as a modest fishing community on the banks of the River Clyde can be dated to the sixth century. Its advantageous position as a commerce hub between the Highlands and the Lowlands helped it develop over time. By the Middle Ages, Glasgow had made a name for itself as a hub of trade, drawing traders from all over Europe.

Glasgow underwent a dramatic development in the 18th century during the Industrial Revolution. The city quickly developed into an industrial powerhouse thanks to its accessibility to iron and coal resources as well as its well-connected canals. Its economy was based on shipbuilding, textiles, and heavy engineering, which caused a population boom as people from the countryside moved to the city in search of work.

Glasgow's skyline saw a significant transformation as the 19th century progressed due to the construction of impressive Victorian structures and other architectural wonders. The city's look was forever changed by the legendary architect Charles Rennie Mackintosh, who fused Scottish design sensibilities with Art Nouveau. Glasgow also had a significant impact on the abolitionist movement at this time, with abolitionists like Frederick Douglass speaking out against slavery in Glasgow's public forums.

Glasgow experienced societal issues despite its industrial success. Urban renewal initiatives were finally sparked by the 20th century's reform movements and overcrowded tenements with terrible living conditions. When the city was heavily bombed during World War II, it still managed to recover and thrive, proving the city's fortitude.

Glasgow has reinvented itself as a center for culture and the arts in recent years. Its vibrant music festivals, world-class museums, and diverse arts sector have given it the moniker "UNESCO City of Music." In addition, the city demonstrated its capacity to host significant international events by hosting the Commonwealth Games in 2014.

Glasgow is now the largest city in Scotland and a thriving crossroads of cultures. Its history, which has been distinguished by industrial prowess, social difficulties, and creative expression, has shaped its identity and continues to have an impact on its course. Glasgow continues to be a tribute to the resilient character of a city that has withstood the test of time, with a nod to the past and an eye toward the future.

2.2 Getting To Know The Culture

A fascinating journey that reveals a tapestry made from history, art, music, and various communities is learning about Glasgow's culture. The cultural character of this thriving Scottish city is a harmonic fusion of tradition and modernity, providing a space that is both warm and deeply textured.

Glasgow's rich past lies at the core of its culture. The architecture of the city, from the imposing Victorian structures to the recognizable shipyards along the River Clyde, is clearly influenced by its industrial past. A look into the city's past and its rise to prominence during the Industrial Revolution is provided by exploring these buildings.

Glasgow's famous art institutions are to thank for the city's artistic and creative flourishing. The Kelvingrove Art Gallery and Museum is home to a rich collection that spans continents and centuries and includes everything from European masterpieces to relics from ancient Egypt. The pioneering architect and designer Charles Rennie Mackintosh, whose distinct style made an enduring impression on Glasgow's creative landscape, is honored for his contributions to the city's celebration of innovation.

Another crucial aspect of Glasgow's culture is its music scene. The city's stages vibrate with the sounds of several genres, from traditional folk music to modern indie rock, as it is a UNESCO City of Music. A historical music venue, the Barrowland Ballroom continues to offer events that are popular with both residents and tourists. It has seen performances by legendary performers.

The people of Glasgow are, however, arguably the most alluring feature of its culture. Glaswegians are noted for their friendliness, tenacity, and kindness. By conversing with the locals, one has the chance to experience their distinct humor and lively chats, which are frequently accompanied by a cordial sharing of tales and observations.

Understanding Glasgow's culture also requires a deep understanding of food. The cuisine of the city, which ranges from traditional haggis to contemporary fusion food, demonstrates its multiculturalism and openness to trying new cuisines. To experience the flavors of Scotland and other countries, explore the crowded markets and neighborhood restaurants.

Glasgow's calendar is filled with festivals and events that highlight the city's rich cultural diversity throughout the year. The city's many cultural attractions include the Glasgow International Comedy Festival, West End Festival, and Celtic Connections music festival, to name a few.

2.3 Things To Avoid In Glasgow

While visiting Glasgow provides visitors a lively and enriching experience, there are a few things to avoid to make your trip to this Scottish city joyful and hassle-free.

Unprepared Weather: Rain is a regular companion in Glasgow's unpredictable weather. No of the season, dress appropriately by combining layers and waterproof gear to avoid being caught off guard.

Lack of Awareness of Local Customs: Honor regional traditions and customs. Glaswegians are often nice, but it's still important to be kind and considerate. Be careful not to bring up sensitive subjects or tell improper jokes.

Underestimating Traffic: During rush hours, Glasgow's city center can become crowded. To prevent getting caught in traffic, it is important to take public transit or to map out your driving routes beforehand.

Neglecting Personal Safety: As in any urban setting, it's critical to be watchful and aware of your surroundings, particularly in crowded places or at night. Keep your possessions safe, and refrain from putting expensive things on show.

Ignoring Public Transportation Options: Glasgow offers a reliable bus and subway system for people to go around. Neglecting these alternatives and depending just on cabs or personal vehicles might result in pointless traffic congestion and parking issues.

Missing Out on Local Cuisine: Glasgow has a wide selection of both traditional and contemporary Scottish foods. To enjoy regional specialties like haggis, neeps and tatties, and freshly caught fish, do not stick to your usual cuisines.

Skipping the Arts and Culture: Glasgow has a thriving and diverse cultural scene, with many museums, art galleries, and historical attractions. Avoid skipping the opportunity to discover the city's creative legacy and history.

Overindulgent Partying: Glasgow's nightlife is vibrant and enjoyable, but it's crucial to use caution and moderation when visiting the city's bars and clubs. Overindulgence may result in unfavorable circumstances or health problems.

Tourists may easily navigate Glasgow's distinctive charm and make the most of their visit while avoiding frequent mistakes by remaining knowledgeable and polite.

CHAPTER THREE

Essential Travel Information

3.1 Best Time To Visit

Glasgow, a bustling Scottish city, attracts tourists all year round with its distinctive fusion of history, culture, and scenic beauty. The best time to visit Glasgow relies primarily on your interests and what you intend to experience during your trip, despite the fact that Glasgow's weather can be somewhat unpredictable.

The months of May to September are great for individuals looking for pleasant weather and outdoor activities. Glasgow experiences pleasant weather during this time, with temperatures between 50°F and 65°F (10°C and 18°C). This makes it ideal for enjoying outdoor festivities like the West End Festival or the Glasgow Mela, a multicultural celebration of music, dancing, and food, as well as exploring the city's many parks, including the gorgeous Kelvingrove Park.

Additionally, the longer daylight hours throughout the summer enable tourists to maximize their time. You may get a taste of the local culture by attending outdoor concerts and busy markets in the famed George Square.

Also conveniently located nearby are places like Loch Lomond and the Trossachs National Park, which offer picturesque settings for hiking and water-based activities.

The shoulder seasons of spring (March to May) and fall (September to November) offer a more agreeable atmosphere than the winter months if you're interested in Glasgow's rich history and architecture. It is ideal for exploring famous sites like Glasgow Cathedral, the University of Glasgow, and the Kelvingrove Art Gallery and Museum during these milder months. Additionally, these times are less busy, making your exploration of the city's past and artistic heritage more intimate.

Winter, which lasts from December to February, is less popular for travelers because of the cooler temperatures and shorter days. However, Glasgow's Christmas markets and Hogmanay celebrations can be magical experiences if you're drawn to joyous holiday markets and warm indoor activities. The year-round lively arts and theater culture in the city also provides a break from the chilly weather.

3.2 Getting Around The City

Glasgow is a city filled with attractions and culture, and getting around is easy thanks to the range of transit choices available. Glasgow offers a variety of options for getting around, including effective public transportation, practical taxis, and walking trails.

Glasgow's comprehensive public transit system is one of the most economical ways to tour the city. The Glasgow Subway, sometimes known as the "Clockwork Orange," runs in a circle connecting the main attractions in the city. With a flat fare and reasonably priced daily passes, the subway is not only a cost-effective choice but also a speedy and effective mode of transportation.

The bus system is yet another essential component of Glasgow's public transit system. Buses, which are run by numerous businesses, offer comprehensive coverage throughout the city and its outskirts. Bus fares are inexpensive, and day passes allow for unlimited travel, making them the best option for travelers who want to visit several places in one day.

Taxis and ride-sharing services like Uber are widely available for people who prefer a more individualized way of transportation. Taxis may cost a little bit more than other modes of transportation, but they are more convenient and take you directly to your destination.

Taxis are particularly helpful when traveling in a large company or with large amounts of stuff.

Glasgow's appeal is also a result of its walkability. The city core is small, and a lot of the attractions are close to one another. Walking around and taking in the neighborhood ambience will also help you find hidden treasures and unforeseen discoveries.

With designated bike lanes and shared routes, Glasgow is becoming a more bicycle-friendly city for aficionados. Renting a bike gives you a fresh viewpoint on the city and enables independent exploration. The cost of renting a bike varies according to how long it will be used.

Glasgow's transportation costs can be roughly estimated as follows when creating a daily budget:

For unlimited use of public transportation (subway/bus), day passes cost between £5 and £10.

Taxi/Uber: depending on distance, fares range from £5 to £20.

Rent a bike for £10–20 per day.

Walking is a cheap and convenient way to explore the city center.

Glasgow provides a variety of transportation choices to accommodate different needs and tastes. Whether you decide to stroll to experience the local culture, take public transportation to learn about the city's history, or take a taxi for convenience, traveling around Glasgow is a simple and delightful experience that enables you to fully enjoy your stay.

3.3 Currency And Money Matters

To ensure a simple and hassle-free trip to Glasgow, it is crucial to be aware of local financial practices and the currency. The British Pound Sterling, also known as the pound (£) or GBP, is the official currency of Glasgow as well as the rest of Scotland and the United Kingdom.

You have many options in Glasgow for handling money and managing your finances. In several locations throughout the city, ATMs (Automated Teller Machines) allow you to withdraw money in pounds using your debit or credit card. To avoid any problems using your cards abroad, it is advisable to let your bank know about your vacation plans. It's a good idea to verify with your bank in advance because some ATMs can charge a fee for using a foreign card.

The majority of establishments in Glasgow, including hotels, restaurants, stores, and attractions, accept credit and debit cards. To be safe, it's a good idea to keep a modest quantity of cash on hand for markets or tiny local merchants who might not accept cards. In the city, contactless payments are also well-liked because they let you complete quick and safe transactions for minor goods.

In Glasgow, leaving a gratuity is traditional while eating out or using other services. Although it's not required, leaving a tip of between 10% and 15% of the total cost is thought to be courteous if you're happy with the service. Before giving a further tip, make sure to check the bill since certain restaurants may contain a service charge.

In Glasgow's city center and nearby, as well as at the airport, you may find bureaux de change and currency exchange offices if you need to convert money. To be sure you're getting a fair price, it's a good idea to compare exchange rates and costs.

The pound notes issued by Scottish banks (such the Royal Bank of Scotland and Clydesdale Bank) are generally recognised throughout the UK, despite the fact that Scotland has its own independent legal currency. You can use them in larger businesses or exchange them for Bank of England notes if you think some locations in England won't accept them.

Overall, managing your money wisely while visiting Glasgow will enable you to concentrate on taking advantage of the city's rich culture, history, and attractions. This includes knowing the local currency, using ATMs and cards, and being aware of tipping norms.

3.4 Language And Communication

Glasgow, a thriving and multicultural city in Scotland, has its own distinctive language and manner of speaking that are a reflection of its extensive history and cultural background. Glasgow's main language is English, although you'll notice that the regional accent and terminology can sometimes be difficult for visitors to understand.

The Glasgow accent, sometimes known as the "Glaswegian" accent, is distinguished by its melodious and unique tone. It is renowned for its distinctive intonation patterns and loud rolling "r" sounds. Although people who are not familiar with the dialect may find it initially challenging to comprehend, interacting with locals is often rewarding because they are kind and accommodating.

Glasgow features a number of regional words and slang that may capture your notice in addition to the accent. Commonly used word "wee" denotes "small" or "little." Say, "Can I have a wee cup of tea?" for instance. The word "braw" also means "excellent" or "great." People frequently remark, "That's a beautiful view from up here!" Gaining some familiarity with these phrases will enable you to interact with locals and fully experience the culture.

Glasgow's communication is distinguished by its warmth and friendliness. Whether it's at a café, on the bus, or in the neighborhood bar, people are typically open to talking to strangers. This kind demeanor extends to the vibrant sense of neighborhood in the city, where people frequently converse informally and provide a hand to one another.

It's crucial to be patient and attentive when speaking with Glaswegians, especially if you're not used to the dialect. Never be afraid to ask someone nicely to repeat themselves or to explain what they said if you're having problems understanding them. The majority of locals are more than willing to make accommodations and guarantee clear communication.

CHAPTER FOUR

Top Attractions In Glasgow

4.1 Glasgow Cathedral

Glasgow Cathedral, also known as St. Mungo's Cathedral, is a magnificent example of Scottish architecture and a tribute to the country's long history. This magnificent medieval structure is a representation of Glasgow's spiritual and cultural legacy and is located in the city's center.

The first stone was put for the cathedral in the 12th century, with Bishop John Achaius serving as the patron. The cathedral was built over several centuries, with several architectural styles illustrating the development of Gothic architecture. The west end, finished in the 15th century, demonstrates the intricate craftsmanship of the Perpendicular Gothic style, while the east end, constructed in the 13th century, features early English Gothic elements.

Glasgow Cathedral's beautiful architecture is among its most amazing features. The great choir and the exquisite stained glass windows that fill the interior with a kaleidoscope of hues as sunlight filters through are visible from the towering central nave, which is flanked by enormous stone pillars. The elaborate stone carvings that adorn the cathedral show off the superb craftsmanship of the artisans of the time by depicting biblical themes, saints, and complicated patterns.

The crypt, which houses the tomb of St. Mungo (also known as St. Kentigern), the patron saint of Glasgow, is a notable feature of the cathedral. Both pilgrims and tourists go here to pay respects to the saint who was important to the development of the city's history and Christian identity.

Glasgow Cathedral has endured its fair share of hardships over the years, including the Scottish Reformation and following periods of neglect. However, due to its toughness and the efforts of preservationists, it has continued to be used as a place of worship.

The cathedral now acts as a hub for culture and education in addition to being a place of worship. Its tranquil ambiance, beautiful architecture, and the sense of antiquity that permeates its walls draw tourists from all over the world. Visitors can immerse themselves in the histories of the people who helped to create and preserve it through guided tours that provide insight into the past of the location.

4.2 Kelvingrove Art Gallery And Museum

The Kelvingrove Art Gallery and Museum is a cultural treasure that charms tourists with its rich collection and gorgeous architecture. It is located in Glasgow's charming West End. This venerable establishment, which was founded in 1901 and offers an enthralling voyage through art, history, and the natural sciences, is a must-see attraction for both locals and visitors.

The Kelvingrove Art Gallery and Museum welcomes guests to explore its spectacular galleries and exhibits starting at 10:00 AM. The impressive red sandstone facade of the museum, which is embellished with exquisite carvings and figures, is evidence of the magnificence of Victorian construction. When entering, visitors are greeted by a beautiful central hall with a huge pipe organ and a stunning vaulted ceiling, which sets the stage for the upcoming works of art.

The museum's collection is incredibly diversified, embracing several fields of study and historical periods. Kelvingrove has exhibits on everything from modern art to ancient civilizations. Famous Scottish artists like Samuel Peploe and Francis Cadell are featured in the "Scottish Colourists" exhibition, while the "Natural

History" area enchants visitors with its assortment of fossils and animal exhibits. Rembrandt, Monet, and Van Gogh are among the artists whose works may be found in the "European Art" gallery.

The museum's emphasis on interaction and involvement is one of its most distinctive aspects. Through interactive exhibits and practical exercises, the "Life Gallery" encourages visitors to discover the wonders of the natural world. The "Art Discovery Centre" promotes a closer connection with the creative process by urging visitors to come up close and personal with the artworks.

As Kelvingrove Art Gallery & Museum closes at 5:00 PM, visitors have plenty of time to explore everything that it has to offer. Beyond the exhibitions, the museum's quaint café provides a lovely spot to unwind and consider the discoveries of the day. Visitors can bring a little of Kelvingrove's charm home with them by shopping in the museum store, which is stocked to the brim with distinctive goods and souvenirs.

4.3 The Riverside Museum

On the banks of the River Clyde in Glasgow, Scotland, the Riverside Museum is a cutting-edge architectural wonder and a veritable gold mine of information about the development of technology and transportation. This cutting-edge museum, which opens its doors at 10:00 AM, provides a fascinating look into transportation throughout history, making it a must-see location for both locals and tourists.

The museum's distinctive exterior, which resembles a ship's hull, immediately draws visitors' attention. A massive collection of more than 3,000 objects relating to transportation, including historic automobiles, bicycles, locomotives, and even a tall ship anchored outside, are housed inside the building's sleek and modern facade, which is built of zinc and glass.

The Riverside Museum's interior displays an extraordinary collection of cars and artifacts that trace Glasgow's transportation development. The "Car Wall" offers a historical tour through the history of the automobile through an aesthetically beautiful arrangement of vehicles. With its elaborate ship models and historical items, the "Clyde Room" transports visitors to a time when ships were being built and maritime trade was thriving.

The Riverside Museum is known for its engaging interactive displays that appeal to visitors of all ages. The "Street" is a scaled-down recreation of an ordinary Glasgow street from the early 20th century, replete with stores and vintage cars. Visitors can enter the past through this immersive experience and learn more about daily living in the past. The "Tall Ship," a historic sailing vessel that may be explored inside and out, stands right outside the museum.

The Riverside Museum offers plenty of time for visitors to examine its varied collection and interesting exhibitions before it closes at 5:00 PM. The café at the museum provides a lovely place for unwinding and enjoying refreshments while taking in views of the river. Visitors can take a little of the Riverside's charm home with them thanks to the museum shop, which is stocked with souvenirs and presents with a transportation theme.

4.4 George Square

Glasgow's George Square, a bustling and significant public area that captures the city's rich history and cultural significance, is located in the city's center. This famous square, which bears King George III's name, has developed over time into a hub for community activities, events, and meetings, drawing both residents and visitors.

George Square, which is surrounded by opulent structures and architectural wonders, is a testimony to

Glasgow's Victorian era and exhibits a diverse range of architectural styles. The Glasgow City Chambers, a magnificent example of Victorian architecture with spectacular marble interiors, elaborate staircases, and delicate woodwork, surround the plaza. The City Chambers is a marvel in and of itself, capturing the 19th-century affluence of the city.

The square itself is a hive of activity, holding a variety of festivals and events all year long. George Square is alive with activity, from political protests and cultural events to markets and concerts. Its popularity as a venue for events of various kinds is facilitated by its strategic location and roomy design, further enhancing its standing as an important municipal space.

The enormous equestrian monument of Sir Walter Scott, a well-known Scottish author and historical figure, is one of the square's most distinctive features. The statue honors Scotland's literary heritage and acts as a hub for contemplation and social interaction. Other sculptures and monuments that surround the statue, each with a different tale to tell, add to the square's historical and cultural significance.

In the heart of the busy city streets, George Square offers a tranquil haven with its well-kept green spaces. On its benches, both locals and visitors frequently take a break while admiring the architecture and lively ambiance around them. The square is transformed into a winter wonderland with a spectacular ice rink and Christmas lights during the holiday season, luring families and friends together for festive celebrations.

4.5 The Glasgow Necropolis

The Glasgow Necropolis is a singular and moving example of Victorian-era preoccupation with grandiose cemetery design and memorialization in Scotland. This expansive necropolis, perched on a hill above Glasgow, is a mesmerizing fusion of art, history, and thought, providing a sobering reflection on mortality and the passing of time.

The Glasgow Necropolis, created by architect John Bryce and inaugurated in 1833, was built in response to the city's expanding population and the requirement for a place for the dead to rest. As tourists rise to the site and are met by panoramic views of the city below, its location atop a hill in the eastern portion of Glasgow adds to its allure.

A vast variety of tombs, mausoleums, and monuments that represent a wide spectrum of architectural styles, from neo-Gothic to Egyptian Revival, make up the necropolis. The ornate carvings, statues, and inscriptions that relate the lives of the people interred there serve as heartbreaking reminders of the Victorian preoccupation with symbolism and the afterlife.

The John Knox Monument, a colossal Gothic spire honoring the Scottish Reformer, is one of the necropolis' most notable attractions. The Victorian era's idealized love for history and tradition is embodied in the monument's design, which is reminiscent of medieval cathedrals.

The necropolis is a storehouse of tales and connections to the past in addition to being a location of memorialization. Here are the resting places of numerous prominent people from Glasgow's past, including businessmen, artists, and philanthropists. The names and biographies of persons who once influenced the city's cultural and social scene are encountered by visitors as they meander through the tombstones and gravestones.

Beyond its historical and artistic value, the Glasgow Necropolis offers a tranquil setting for reflection. In the middle of the busy metropolitan environment, its hilltop location creates a sense of peace and tranquility, allowing visitors to take a minute to ponder. Contemplative walks and quiet times can be enjoyed on the wonderfully maintained gardens and winding paths.

4.6 Glasgow Botanic Gardens

The Glasgow Botanic Gardens are a tranquil haven of horticultural brilliance, natural beauty, and scientific inquiry located in Glasgow, Scotland's bustling West End. The botanic gardens have gained popularity as a popular retreat for locals and tourists looking for solace and inspiration because of their extensive collection of plant species, architectural wonders, and educational opportunities.

The Glasgow Botanic Gardens were established in 1817 and have a long, illustrious history. A magnificent glasshouse in the middle of the gardens called The Kibble Palace is a shining example of Victorian engineering and architectural magnificence. Visitors can walk amid exotic plants from all over the world thanks to the fascinating ambiance created by the elaborate ironwork and glass design. A stunning variety of plants, including ferns, towering palms, and tropical species, may be found inside the glasshouse, creating a fascinating sensory experience.

The actual gardens are a gorgeous tapestry of landscapes, each thoughtfully created to highlight a diversity of plant species and ecosystems. Visitors can explore a wide variety of gardens, each with its own special charm, ranging from the serene surroundings of the Main Range to the brilliant hues of the Rose Garden. The Rock Garden has alpine and forest flora in a stunning setting, while the Arboretum displays an extensive collection of mature trees from throughout the world.

The enormous collection of plant species from all parts of the world is one of the highlights of the Glasgow Botanic Gardens. During the flowering season, the renowned Rhododendron Collection, for instance, exhibits a riot of colors, and the Herbaceous Border thrills with a profusion of colorful blooms. The gardens also have themed areas, such the Australian Rainforest Glade and the Mediterranean Garden, giving guests the chance to traverse the world through horticulture.

The goal of the Glasgow Botanic Gardens includes both education and community involvement. All age groups and interests are catered to through the gardens' numerous programs, tours, and events. The gardens offer a venue for education and the development of a closer relationship with nature, hosting everything from botanical art classes to wildlife discovery events.

4.7 The Lighthouse

The Lighthouse, a structure in Glasgow, Scotland, is more than just a structure; it is a symbol of inventiveness, originality, and architectural skill. This famous building, created by renowned architect Charles Rennie Mackintosh, is a representation of Glasgow's artistic legacy and dedication to design quality.

The Lighthouse, which was initially built in the late 19th century as the Glasgow Herald newspaper's headquarters, has undergone a renovation to become a vibrant hub for architecture and design. It welcomes visitors and provides a stimulating selection of exhibits, workshops, and events that honor Scotland's design heritage and motivate younger generations.

The helical staircase, often referred to as the "Mackintosh Tower," is the most recognizable aspect of the Lighthouse. Visitors are treated to breathtaking panoramic views of Glasgow's skyline as this architectural wonder weaves its way higher. With its blend of form and function, the tower honors Mackintosh's imaginative approach to design.

A number of galleries and exhibition rooms that display the development of design, architecture, and art are housed inside The Lighthouse. The "Mackintosh Interpretation Centre" sheds emphasis on Charles Rennie Mackintosh's creative contributions to the field of design by providing insights into his life and work. The "Design Gallery" exhibits current design initiatives and installations, emphasizing the meeting point of creativity and use.

The Lighthouse serves as a centre for education and exploration in addition to being a place for display. The "Education Suite" provides activities for visitors of all ages, including seminars, workshops, and programs that entice them to learn more about architecture and design. A great place to unwind and enjoy the creative ambiance is the "Mackintosh at the Willow" tearoom, a faithful recreation of Mackintosh's original design.

The Lighthouse not only serves as a cultural hub, but it also has a significant impact on the yearly Glasgow International Festival of Visual Art. The festival gathers designers, artists, and other creatives from all over the world, encouraging a thriving interchange of thoughts and pushing the limits of visual expression.

4.8 People's Palace and Winter Gardens

In Glasgow, Scotland, the People's Palace and Winter Gardens are a compelling pair that perfectly capture the social history, cultural legacy, and dedication to civic involvement of the city. This famous relic is tucked away in Glasgow Green Park and offers guests a one-of-a-kind trip through time, exhibiting the lives and tales of Glasgow residents.

Often referred to as the "museum of the people," the People's Palace was built in 1898 with the intention of giving the working-class populace a place to enjoy culture, education, and leisure. With its magnificent glass dome and elaborate ironwork, the museum's architecture captures the grandeur of the Victorian era. A wide variety of objects, images, and exhibits that span Glasgow's social history from the late 18th century to the present day are housed inside the People's Palace.

The museum's displays give visitors a look into the difficulties, victories, and everyday lives of Glaswegians throughout time. The People's Palace creates a vivid portrait of urban life, resiliency, and the sense of community that defines Glasgow, with recreations of a historic Glasgow street and interactive displays illustrating the city's industrial background.

The Winter Gardens, a gorgeous glasshouse housing a luscious and varied assortment of plants from all over the world, is located next to the People's Palace. The Winter Gardens, which were created as a Victorian conservatory, offer a peaceful respite from the hustle and bustle of the city by encouraging guests to meander amid botanical wonders and enjoy the sights, sounds, and tranquility of a tropical oasis.

The People's Palace and the Winter Gardens work together to create a seamless fusion of nature, culture, and history. To promote a deeper understanding of Glasgow's social structure and development, The People's Palace provides a multitude of educational programs, workshops, and exhibitions that are appropriate for all age groups. The Winter Gardens, meanwhile, offer a beautiful backdrop for unwinding, thinking, and appreciating nature.

Glasgow's cultural scene is significantly shaped by the People's Palace and the Winter Gardens, which hold a range of occasions, performances, and festivals all year long. This dynamic pair acts as a hub for the artistic expression and sense of community in the city, hosting everything from art exhibitions and craft fairs to live music and social events.

CHAPTER FIVE

Exploring Neighborhoods

5.1 City Centre

Glasgow's City Centre is a bustling center that captures the rich fabric of Scotland's history, culture, and contemporary vibrancy. It is tucked away along the banks of the River Clyde. When you explore this area, you'll find a fascinating fusion of stunning architectural wonders, world-class museums, hopping marketplaces, and a vibrant arts scene that captures the soul of the city.

The variety of buildings in Glasgow's City Center is one of its most notable characteristics. The magnificent Glasgow Cathedral, built in the 12th century, is a testimony to medieval engineering, and the Riverside Museum, a modern wonder, highlights the city's history as a center of shipbuilding. Walking down Buchanan Street displays grandeur from the Victorian era, with elaborate buildings and grand shopping arcades that make it a haven for those who want retail therapy.

The abundance of museums and galleries that dot the City Centre will fascinate culture fans. Both locals and visitors should visit the Kelvingrove Art Gallery and

Museum since it includes a diverse collection of artworks, antiquities, and natural history exhibitions. The People's Palace provides a window into Glaswegians' lives throughout the centuries for people interested in learning more about Scotland's industrial past.

The Glasgow Royal Concert Hall and the Theatre Royal, where top-notch performances of music, drama, and dance frequently take place, help to fuel the City Centre's thriving cultural sector. The Glasgow Film Theatre in the area appeals to cinephiles with its carefully chosen collection of independent and foreign films.

Without sampling Glasgow's delectable cuisine, no exploration of the city is complete. The City Center is home to a wide variety of restaurants, from cutting-edge cafes that are pushing the boundaries of cuisine to classic Scottish pubs offering substantial haggis. Visitors can have a whiskey dram in one of the numerous old pubs or indulge in international cuisine in the hip Merchant City neighborhood.

Glasgow's City Centre has areas of peace in addition to the urban bustle. One of the city's oldest public parks, the tranquil Glasgow Green offers a haven from the busy streets. For visitors wishing to unwind, its expansive lawns, walking lanes, and historical landmarks provide a tranquil haven.

5.2 West End

Glasgow's West End, which is tucked away to the west of the city center, emits an irresistible aura of bohemian charm and creative energy. A must-visit location for those looking for an immersive and energetic experience, this unique neighborhood is a mesmerizing blend of old architecture, leafy avenues, cultural destinations, and a booming food scene.

The astonishing mix of the West End's architectural styles is one of its defining characteristics. The University of Glasgow, which was established in 1451, is a magnificent example of the area's historical significance. A stunning backdrop is created by its neo-Gothic spires and finely carved stone facades. Victorian and Edwardian townhouses abound in the Kelvingrove Park neighborhood, providing a window into Glasgow's architectural development.

The Kelvingrove Art Gallery and Museum is the focal point of the West End's vibrant arts and cultural scene. It is a treasure trove for art lovers, housing a diverse assortment of artworks, antiquities, and historical displays. A wonderful collection of artistic and scientific marvels is on display close by at the Hunterian Museum, offering a distinctive viewpoint on the world.

For artists and creators, the West End is a refuge. The quaint cluster of studios and workshops known as The Hidden Lane is proof of the area's dedication to promoting artistic expression. Here, guests may see artists at work and perhaps even buy a unique item to keep as a souvenir.

The West End has a variety of culinary establishments that can satisfy every palate, so foodies are in for a treat. There is something to satiate every craving, from tiny cafes serving artisanal coffee to multinational eateries serving up world delicacies. The Byres Road neighborhood is particularly well-known for its gastronomic diversity, providing a delicious tour of international flavors.

The vast Kelvingrove Park, one of many green spaces in the West End, is a haven for pleasure. Its verdant meadows, winding paths, and breathtaking views of the River Kelvin make it the ideal location for a tranquil picnic or leisurely stroll.

The lively energy of the West End permeates all of its occasions and celebrations, including the West End Festival, which honors regional music, art, and culture. The area comes alive all year long with live concerts, markets, and community events that highlight its vibrant culture.

5.3 Merchant City

A charming blend of traditional charm and contemporary sophistication may be found in Glasgow's Merchant City area. This historic area, which served as the city's commercial and trading center in its heyday, has evolved into a thriving cultural neighborhood. A tour through cobblestone streets, artistic treasures, culinary delights, and a buzzing atmosphere that encapsulates Glasgow's past and present is provided by exploring Merchant City.

The architecture of Merchant City is a living testament to its past. The opulent façade of ancient warehouses and trading houses transport us to the city's prosperous commercial past, while the atmospheric High Street displays buildings that date back hundreds of years. Due to the buildings that have been transformed into chic boutiques, art galleries, and cafes, the historic Trongate and Wilson Street nevertheless have a feeling of the past.

Merchant City is a refuge for creativity because art and culture are in vogue there. The Gallery of Modern Art (GoMA), which houses a varied collection of works that defy expectations and elicit contemplation, is a shining example of contemporary artistic expression. The lively location for exhibitions, performances, and talks that push the limits of artistic exploration is close by at the Centre for Contemporary Arts (CCA).

The festivals and events in the neighborhood are a part of the area's vibrant cultural scene. The neighborhood is transformed into a colorful stage for live music, street performances, and artistic installations during the annual spectacular known as the Merchant City Festival. This creative festival draws both locals and tourists, establishing a sense of community.

The variety of restaurants located throughout Merchant City will satisfy even the most discerning palates. The area offers a gourmet experience that appeals to a variety of preferences, from stylish bistros to international restaurants. The thriving street food markets, including the Briggait Farmers' Market, highlight regionally produced artisanal goods and locally sourced ingredients.

Merchant City doesn't let down those looking for peace and quiet and greenery. While the gorgeous Glasgow Green offers spacious lawns, strolling trails, and historic monuments for a leisurely outdoor experience, the Italian Centre's courtyard offers a calm respite from the city's bustle.
Both locals and visitors find Merchant City to be a charming place thanks to its fusion of history and

modern elegance. Its bustling streets beckon investigation of its distinctive stores, art galleries, and restaurants. Merchant City offers a memorable experience that captures the spirit of Glasgow's history and present, whether you're indulging in a cultural immersion, tasting great cuisine, or simply taking in the atmosphere of this vibrant neighborhood.

5.4 Finnieston

Finnieston, a neighborhood in Glasgow that is tucked away on the banks of the River Clyde, has quickly grown to be one of the city's most active and sought-after areas. This formerly industrial area has seen an amazing makeover, becoming a hip and varied neighborhood that fuses its industrial past with a modern flair. When you explore Finnieston, you'll find an enticing fusion of fine restaurants, creative treasures, and a buzzing atmosphere that has given the area a reputation as the hippest neighborhood in the city.

Finnieston's architecture reflects its industrial background, and the ruins of old warehouses and factories offer a window into the city's past. The tall remnant of the shipbuilding era known as the Finnieston Crane is a testimony to the neighborhood's maritime history. This graphic narrative depicts the growth of

Finnieston and contrasts these industrial artifacts with contemporary constructions.

Finnieston's thriving culinary industry is one of its most distinctive aspects, making it a haven for foodies. The neighborhood's main thoroughfare, Argyle Street, is lined with a variety of eateries, from quaint cafes to elegant restaurants. There are numerous dining alternatives in Finnieston's "Foodie Quarter" that cover a wide range of international cuisines, offering a delicious adventure for every palate. With creative menus and products produced locally, the region has emerged as a hub for culinary innovation.

Finnieston is a dynamic community where art and culture are in vogue, with studios and galleries adding to the atmosphere. Featuring exhibitions, live performances, and other activities that honor artistic expression in all of its manifestations, SWG3 is a multidisciplinary arts complex. Visitors can find peace and make connections with both nature and art at Tramway's Hidden Gardens, a calm haven tucked away inside the grounds.

The dynamic atmosphere of Finnieston is heightened by its events and festivals. The Mardi Gras Parade of the West End Festival weaves through the streets of the neighborhood, giving it a carnival-like ambiance.

Additionally, the eagerly anticipated EatFilm event creates a distinctive and immersive experience by fusing movie screenings with food delights.

The Riverside Museum's surroundings offer picturesque views of the River Clyde and plenty of possibilities for leisurely strolls, which is one of the many green places that contribute to Finnieston's appeal. The scenic waterside walkways along the Clydeside Promenade are ideal for admiring the breathtaking sunsets that brighten the Glasgow skyline.

5.5 Southside

Glasgow's Southside is a community distinguished by its rich diversity, historic charm, and strong feeling of community. It is tucked away just south of the River Clyde. The Southside provides a distinctive and genuine Glasgow experience that is often overshadowed by its busier peers, making it well worth investigating. The Southside offers a tapestry of culture, legacy, and companionship that captivates the heart of the city, from its beautiful parks to its bustling local markets.

The diversity of the Southside's architecture is one of its defining characteristics. The magnificent tenements made of sandstone that line its streets are a throwback to

Glasgow's Victorian era. The Pollokshields Conservation Area is a hidden gem of lavish houses and tree-lined streets that showcase the wealth of a bygone period. On the other hand, the Govan region is home to historical sites like the over a thousand-year-old Govan Old Parish Church, which serves as a reminder of the area's rich history.

The Southside is a vibrant center for art and culture, with places like the Tramway acting as a dynamic gathering place for exhibits, performances, and joint artistic endeavors. The cultural institutions in the neighborhood, such the Burrell Collection, are home to an extraordinary collection of works of art and artifacts that illustrate Glasgow's connections to other countries. An annual celebration of creativity, the Southside Fringe Festival brings together regional performers, musicians, and artists in a vibrant and diversified presentation.

In the Southside, where a wide variety of restaurants cater to different tastes and preferences, culinary exploration is a joy. A delightful fusion of flavors from around the world may be found at the cosmopolitan dining establishments that line the busy Victoria Road. The dining options in the Southside reflect the diversity of the neighborhood, ranging from traditional Scottish fare to exotic international cuisine.

Local markets and events serve as prime examples of the Southside's strong feeling of community. The Queen's Park Farmers' Market is a bustling gathering place where locals and visitors alike congregate to celebrate locally made items. It is located in the center of Queen's Park. The Queen's Park Arena hosts activities, performances, and outdoor movies that promote community spirit and are representative of the area.

The Southside has grassy spots that offer comfort and peace amidst its metropolitan environment. One of Glasgow's oldest parks, Queen's Park, offers tranquil walkways, a boating pond, and sweeping views of the city skyline from its famous flagpole. In addition, Pollok Country Park is a lush refuge that is home to the magnificent Pollok House and a herd of Highland cattle and offers a tranquil respite from the bustle of the city.

CHAPTER SIX

Outdoor Activities And Parks

6.1 Glasgow Green

Glasgow Green, which is located along the banks of the River Clyde, is a tribute to the city's lengthy history, rich cultural legacy, and transformation into a thriving urban oasis. This large public park, which spans 136 acres, is not only one of the oldest in the city but also a beloved gathering place for both residents and visitors.

Glasgow Green, which dates to the 15th century, has undergone numerous changes. It began as a grazing area but eventually developed into a hub for celebrations, markets, and political gatherings. The legendary Doulton Fountain, a magnificent Victorian monument covered in elaborate porcelain panels depicting British colonies and dominions, serves as a focal point for its historical significance.

The People's Palace and Winter Gardens stand out among the verdant foliage and tranquil surroundings. This elegant museum presents the experiences of Glasgow's working-class residents and sheds light on the socioeconomic history of the city. No of the season, the nearby Winter Gardens, a glasshouse packed with exotic plants, provides a peaceful haven.

Numerous cultural celebrations and activities have taken place on Glasgow Green. The Glasgow Fair, which celebrates the city's love of carnival rides, games, and fireworks, has a history spanning centuries and annually gathers music lovers from all over the world.

Due to the park's close vicinity to the River Clyde, guests may enjoy the river's breathtaking views and its significance to the city's industrial past. A symbolic entrance to the park and the history of the city is provided by the McLennan Arch, a piece of the ancient city gate.

Football fields, tennis courts, and even a skatepark are available for sports fans, inviting both recreational athletes and serious sports enthusiasts to participate in friendly tournaments or relaxing activities.

6.2 Pollok Country Park

A lush haven tucked away in Glasgow's hectic city center, Pollok Country Park provides a tranquil haven with the ideal fusion of recreation, history, and the natural world. This expansive urban sanctuary, which spans over 360 acres of lush landscapes, woodlands, and meadows, is a tribute to the city's dedication to maintaining its natural beauty.

The famous Pollok House, a stately Georgian home, resides in this park that expertly blends history and culture. Explore the magnificent chambers of the estate, which are decorated with antique furnishings, art collections, and stunning architecture and offer a window into the wealthy Maxwell family's former lifestyle.

The park's unique fauna and habitats are among its main draws. With its charming river and waterfall, the Old Pollok Glen creates the perfect environment for leisurely strolls and quiet reflection. The park's vast woodlands are home to a variety of plants and animals, making it a refuge for birdwatchers and other nature lovers.

Pollok Country Park provides a variety of activities for families and outdoor lovers. Beautiful riverfront walkways for leisurely walks, jogging, or cycling may be found along the Riverside Garden and Clydeside Walkway. The park's large green spaces are ideal for outdoor meetings, picnics, and frisbee games, and the adventure playground is fun for kids.

The Burrell Collection, a renowned art collection given to the city by Sir William Burrell, will thrill art enthusiasts. The collection is housed in a contemporary structure tucked away inside the park and includes a diverse range of artworks, including sculptures, tapestries, and paintings from various centuries and civilizations.

Pollok Country Park is a beloved getaway that develops a closer relationship with environment and history, not just a place for recreation. Those seeking consolation in the middle of modernity might find rest and renewal in its peaceful coexistence with the city's urban fabric. Visitors to Pollok Country Park are guaranteed to find a mesmerizing sanctuary that captures Glasgow's multidimensional beauty, whether they are discovering its cultural treasures, savoring the serenity of its natural landscapes, or simply spending a leisurely day outside.

6.3 The Botanic Gardens

The Botanic Gardens are a hidden gem of botanical wonder and natural beauty in the middle of Glasgow. This verdant sanctuary, which covers 27 acres, has been enthralling tourists for more than 200 years with its extensive collection of plants, tranquil surroundings, and eye-catching exhibits.

The Botanic Gardens, which were first built in 1817, have grown to be a veritable treasure trove of plant varieties. Each portion of the garden, which is divided into many themed sections, provides a distinct and engrossing experience. As a spectacular focal point, the Kibble Palace, a magnificent glasshouse, shelters exotic plants from various climatic zones, including palms, ferns, and tropical blossoms.

The glasshouses stretch to the Main Range, built in the Victorian era, which is home to a wide variety of cactus, carnivorous plants, and orchids. A variety of palms and cycads are shown in the recently constructed Temperate Palm House in a controlled setting that resembles their native habitats.

Visitors are greeted to a riot of colors and scents as they stroll through the charming Herbaceous Border, and in the spring, the Rhododendron Walk puts on a spectacular show of these colorful blooms. The Rose Garden is a romantic getaway for couples and a favored location for photographers because of its beautiful patterns and delightful scents.

The Botanic Gardens' tranquillity extends to its arboretum, where a varied assortment of trees and shrubs makes a calm setting for leisurely strolls. While the Children's Garden stimulates young explorers with interactive displays and educational activities, a meandering trail along the River Kelvin offers an opportunity to get close to nature.

The gardens are naturally beautiful, but they also offer a variety of events, workshops, and exhibitions all year round. The Botanic Gardens cultivate a sense of community and offer opportunities for learning and interaction through botanical art classes, garden tours, and seasonal festivals.

6.4 Loch Lomond

Loch Lomond, which is tucked away inside the stunning scenery of the Trossachs National Park, represents Scotland's natural beauty and attractiveness in a spectacular way. Loch Lomond, which is nearly 24 miles long and is the largest freshwater loch in Great Britain, is known for its peaceful waters, lush hills, and craggy mountains.

Poets, painters, and visitors have been moved by the loch's distinctive beauty for generations. The magnificent peaks of the Ben Lomond mountain surround its northern banks, and its southern portions are ornamented with charming towns and verdant woodlands. Outdoor enthusiasts will find the surrounding landscape to be a haven for activities like hiking, mountain biking, and water sports like kayaking, fishing, and sailing.

Each of the interconnecting islands in the lake has its own distinct charm. The largest island, Inchmurrin, has forests, hiking paths, and even an ancient castle ruin. Inchcailloch is a designated National Nature Reserve and is recognized for its unique flora and wildlife. It provides chances for birdwatching and forest and meadow exploration.

The varied character of Loch Lomond along its length is one of its most striking characteristics. The southern expanses open up to greater vistas and serene bays, while the tight, northern section is flanked by sheer mountain slopes and exudes a sense of grandeur. With its lovely cottages and well-preserved heritage, the picturesque village of Luss on the loch's western beaches provides a look into traditional Scottish life.

The areas around the loch are not just a haven for nature lovers, but also a center of culture. A variety of services, lodging options, and attractions, including the Loch Lomond Shores complex, are available to visitors in the nearby town of Balloch, which serves as the entrance to Loch Lomond and Trossachs National Park.

The West Highland Way, a long-distance trail that circles around Loch Lomond's eastern shore and provides hikers with a memorable journey across diverse landscapes, adds to the loch's attraction.

6.5 The Trossachs National Park

The Trossachs National Park is a vast tapestry of craggy mountains, clean lochs, lush woods, and quaint villages that is nestled in the center of Scotland. This magnificent wilderness, which covers an area of more than 720 square miles, serves as a living example of Scotland's natural splendor and rich cultural history.

The Trossachs, sometimes known as the "Highlands in Miniature," offer a wide variety of scenery that pique the interest of tourists. The serene waters of Loch Katrine, Loch Lomond, and Loch Venachar reflect the shifting moods of the sky, while towering summits like Ben Lomond and Ben A'an offer breathtaking panoramic views.

A trip through time and history can be had by exploring the park. The word "Trossachs," which refers to the region, is Gaelic for "bristly territory," a reference to the once-dense trees that covered it. Red deer, ospreys, and golden eagles can all find refuge in the park's historic woodland remains, which are still there today.

The history of Scotland is also entwined with that of the Trossachs National Park. Legendary Scottish folk hero Rob Roy MacGregor formerly roamed these territories, leaving a legacy that still piques tourists' interest. The park's tranquil vistas and evocative glens have served as an inspiration to poets and writers, including Sir Walter Scott, who gave the area literary immortality.

The Trossachs provide outdoor enthusiasts with a playground for exploration. All skill levels can enjoy the park's many hiking and mountain biking paths. One of Scotland's most well-known long-distance trails, the West Highland Way, winds through the park, providing hikers with a completely immersed experience. Visitors can interact with the lochs and rivers that wind through the terrain by participating in water sports like kayaking, canoeing, and fishing.

Charming towns and villages like Callander and Aberfoyle encourage exploration and offer a taste of the way of life there. Ceilidh dances, Highland games, and music festivals all provide opportunities to experience the vivacious Scottish spirit.

CHAPTER SEVEN

Arts and Culture

7.1 Theatre Scene

Glasgow's theater industry is a thriving and dynamic cultural landscape that has won the hearts of both locals and tourists. Glasgow's theater scene, which is renowned for its extensive history, wide range of productions, and enthusiastic community, is proof of the city's dedication to the arts.

The city is home to a broad variety of theaters, each with its own distinct personality and schedule. Glasgow's theatrical tradition is anchored by the opulent Victorian King's Theatre. It attracts audiences of all ages by presenting a variety of classic plays, modern performances, and musicals. The Citizens Theatre, on the other hand, is praised for its provocative plays and creative narrative techniques. It was founded in 1943 and has a history of fostering new talent and extending the possibilities of dramatic expression.

The theatre scene in Glasgow is not limited to conventional theaters. In a former cathedral, the Tron Theatre now serves as a center for unconventional and independent shows. It offers a stage for up-and-coming performers and presents innovative performances that defy expectations. The Theatre Royal also offers a wide variety of shows, from West End successes to ballet and opera, to suit a variety of creative preferences.

Glasgow's theater culture cannot be discussed without mentioning its festivals and events. The Glasgow International Comedy Festival, which features top-notch comics from all around the world, makes the city chuckle. Even while the Glasgow Film Festival is largely focused on movies, it frequently include live shows and other activities that mix theater and movies.

Glasgow's theater scene is a close-knit and encouraging network. To give viewers engrossing experiences, local playwrights, directors, designers, and actors work together. Beyond live performances, educational initiatives, workshops, and masterclasses make sure that the city's love of theatre is passed down to future generations.

7.2 Music Venues

Glasgow has a reputation as a haven for music lovers thanks to its vibrant and thrilling music scene. Glasgow's music scene is a symphony of creativity and passion, with a rich history, a wide range of genres, and recognizable venues.

The city's renowned music venues are at the center of this musical tapestry. The Barrowland Ballroom is a well-known representation of Glasgow's musical heritage. With a colorful past that stretches back to the 1930s, it has played host to a number of iconic performers, including David Bowie and Nirvana. It is a beloved location for both artists and spectators due to the intimate setting, distinctive architecture, and palpable energy.

Since its debut in 2013, the SSE Hydro, a technological marvel, has quickly established itself as one of Europe's top concert venues. Top-tier international musicians have been drawn to Glasgow by its cutting-edge facilities and capacity to hold over 13,000 guests, ensuring that it continues to be a stop on many world tours.

King Tut's Wah Wah Hut is a moniker that is connected with up-and-coming talent for a more personal encounter. As the birthplace of bands like Oasis, this little but legendary venue has a talent for seeing the future's biggest talents. Its intimate atmosphere and legacy of supporting ground-breaking performers generate an unmatched connection between artists and their audience.

Glasgow's music culture is thriving both inside and outside of conventional venues. Classical orchestras and contemporary artists play in a variety of settings at the Glasgow Royal Concert Hall. From rock to hip-hop, the O2 Academy Glasgow provides a stage for artists from a variety of genres, making sure that every musical preference is catered to.

The music scene in Glasgow is also greatly influenced by music festivals. The hugely popular TRNSMT Festival pulls some of the biggest names in the industry to Glasgow Green. The city's dedication to conserving and advancing its musical history is further demonstrated at Celtic Connections, a festival of folk and traditional music.

7.3 Street Art And Murals

Glasgow's streets are a colorful canvas that, via its alluring street art and murals, portrays a story of artistic freedom, innovation, and cultural diversity. The city has turned its open areas into outdoor exhibition spaces, inviting inhabitants and tourists to enjoy its dynamic urban environment.

Glasgow's street art community is distinguished by its diverse range of themes and techniques. The famous "St.

Mungo" mural by artist Smug, which honors the city's patron saint and catches the imagination with its complex intricacies and brilliant colors, is one of the most recognizable works. Similar to this, Rogue-One's "Honey, I Shrunk the Kids" painting lends a whimsical touch to the city by showing exaggerated insects and other creatures that jokingly interact with the surrounding structures.

Additionally, the city's walls are a living record of provocative social and political commentary. Muralists like Rogue-One, Adele Renault, and Klingatron use their art to address significant themes like climate change, inequality, and mental health, challenging preconceptions and igniting discussions between art and society.

Glasgow is well-known not only for its individual murals but also for its designated street art places. For instance, the SWG3 Yard has changing murals and art works that add to the city's dynamic urban image. In the meantime, the Barras Art and Design Centre (BAaD) presents a distinctive fusion of creative studios, markets, and occasions that honor the artistic character of the city.

Glasgow has a thriving street art community that is spread throughout the entire city. The Mural Trail leads visitors through several communities while revealing a variety of stunning works of art at every turn. This self-guided trip allows tourists to explore Glasgow beyond its well-known sights and offers a window into the artistic essence of the city.

The city's acceptance of artistic expression as a means of reviving public places and promoting a feeling of community is ultimately demonstrated through Glasgow's street art and murals. Glasgow's streets come to life as a living, breathing monument to the ability of art to inspire, provoke, and unify through the lens of these colorful murals.

7.4 Festivals And Events

Glasgow, a city known for its thriving arts community, is home to a wide variety of festivals and events that honor everything from food and literature to music and the arts. These energetic events highlight the city's vibrant spirit and provide both locals and guests with life-changing experiences.

Glasgow attracts a lot of music lovers because of its top-notch events. For a series of concerts, workshops, and performances, musicians from all over the world come together as part of the Celtic Connections Festival, an international celebration of folk and traditional music.

This event celebrates Scotland's rich musical legacy while also showcasing its linkages to other countries.

One of the top music festivals in the UK, TRNSMT Festival has grown quickly in stature. The Glasgow Green setting attracts great performers and devoted spectators for an exhilarating weekend of music. TRNSMT epitomizes the city's modern music culture and its capacity to appeal to a wide range of preferences with a diversified program covering genres from rock to pop.

Glasgow Film Festival offers a well curated collection of foreign and domestic films that appeals to film enthusiasts. Along with screenings, the festival frequently hosts seminars, special events, and Q&A sessions with directors and actors to engage movie fans and provide a forum for thought-provoking debates.

Literary enthusiasts are not forgotten, as the Aye Write! Renowned writers, poets, and intellectuals congregate at the Glasgow Book Festival for stimulating conversations and captivating presentations. This festival promotes intellectual curiosity while highlighting the city's literary heritage.

Laughter and joy are delivered on stage by local and international comedians throughout the Glasgow

International Comedy Festival, much to the delight of foodies. It's a monument to Glasgow's sense of humor and capacity for cultivating environments that encourage group hilarity and good humor.

Glasgow's ancient Merchant City neighborhood is transformed into a thriving center of creativity by the Merchant City Festival. This event perfectly captures the city's dedication to preserving its creative and cultural traditions, with street performances, visual art exhibits, live music, and markets.

In addition to this, Glasgow celebrates occasions honoring dance, the visual arts, LGBTQ+ pride, and more, reflecting its inclusive and diverse spirit. These festivals and events highlight the city's changing identity as a major worldwide cultural hub, foster community interaction, and add to its liveliness.

CHAPTER EIGHT

Shopping And Dining

8.1 Buchanan Street Shopping

In the center of Glasgow, Scotland, Buchanan Street is a thriving and busy shopping district that has established a reputation as one of the best shopping streets in the UK. Buchanan Street, which spans several city blocks, is a mesmerizing fusion of old-world beauty and modern commerce that draws both locals and visitors.

The street's stunning architecture is what first draws people in. A spectacular collection of Victorian and Edwardian structures along Buchanan Street, with elaborate facades and decorative embellishments that pay homage to Glasgow's former industrial heyday. These stunning examples of architecture provide as a mesmerizing backdrop for the wide range of retail establishments that make Buchanan Street a shoppers' haven.

Shopaholics can browse an outstanding selection of upscale shops, department stores, and well-known brands. The street is anchored by the renowned Buchanan Galleries, a multi-level shopping complex that houses numerous fashion, lifestyle, and technology retailers. The House of Fraser offers a carefully chosen collection of designer labels for affluent customers, while Buchanan Street's independent boutiques provide a distinctive shopping experience with one-of-a-kind apparel, accessories, and crafts.

Additionally, Buchanan Street is a culinary mecca. Charming cafes, bistros, and restaurants that serve a variety of world cuisines and Scottish fare are tucked away amid the stores. Indulging in a delicious lunch while taking a break from retail therapy adds to the street's appeal as a multifaceted destination.

The cultural importance of the Boulevard goes beyond only its use for dining and shopping. An energetic setting that appeals to all the senses is created by street performers, musicians, and artists. The frequently hosted Buchanan Street Market features regional producers and craftsmen, enabling guests to bring a bit of Glasgow's ingenuity home.

The accessibility of Buchanan Street increases its allure. It is conveniently accessible by public transit, making it simple for guests to travel there from different areas of the city. The pedestrian-friendly layout of the street encourages leisurely strolls and allows customers to browse at their own pace.

8.2 The Barras Market

The Barras Market, a cultural icon and haven for visitors looking for a genuine shopping experience, is tucked away in Glasgow's East End. The Barras has grown from its modest origins into a bustling marketplace that offers a broad array of goods, ranging from old treasures to fresh vegetables and everything in between, thanks to its rich history and dynamic ambiance.

The Barras Market, which opened in the early 20th century, has remained true to itself over time. Visitors can browse a diverse selection of goods in a lively and dynamic environment created by the market's outdoor vendors and covered arcades. The market offers a vast variety of goods that appeal to many different tastes and interests, making it a gold mine for collectors and bargain hunters alike. These goods range from antiques, apparel, and electronics to books, crafts, and bric-a-brac.

The Barras is distinguished by its genuine and welcoming atmosphere. A friendly and neighborhood-focused ambiance is created by the market's proprietors and vendors, many of whom have been involved for decades. This personal touch improves the shopping experience by enabling customers to interact with vendors who are enthusiastic about their goods and frequently willing to share tales about The Barras' past.

The market's vintage sector, where collectors can find one-of-a-kind and unusual objects from bygone eras, is one of its highlights. Some of the hidden gems include vinyl recordings, vintage clothing, antique furniture, and odd artifacts. This area of The Barras draws visitors looking for a nostalgic trip down memory lane as well as collectors.

The Barras is a cultural center that features live entertainment, musical performances, and a variety of food booths in addition to shopping. Visitors can indulge in a variety of international cuisines and regional specialties while experiencing a sensory journey that goes beyond simple shopping.

The Barras' convenient placement near other noteworthy sights including the famed music venue Barrowland Ballroom adds to its charm. Its central location and ease of access by public transportation make it a must-visit for both residents and visitors hoping to experience Glasgow's true spirit.

8.3 Culinary Scene And Local Delicacies

With a combination of traditional Scottish flavors and foreign influences, Glasgow, the largest city in Scotland, has established itself as a vibrant and diversified culinary destination. Glasgow offers a gourmet experience that celebrates both regional tradition and international innovation thanks to its expanding food scene and abundance of dining alternatives.

Scottish breakfast is one of the most recognizable foods that best represents Glasgow's culinary identity. This filling dish is generally served with baked beans, mushrooms, and grilled tomatoes along with bacon, sausages, black pudding, haggis, eggs, and tattie scones (potato scones). A fantastic introduction to the city's appreciation of robust, savory foods, this feast is.

The traditional Scottish dish haggis is a must-try while visiting Glasgow. Haggis, a dish made of minced sheep's offal, onions, oats, suet, and spices, is traditionally cooked inside a sheep's stomach. Modern adaptations are frequently served with neeps and tatties (mashed turnips and potatoes), but without the casing. Particularly when taken part in a Burns Supper celebration, it is not just a culinary event but also a cultural one.

Glasgow's culinary scene is a mash-up of international influences in addition to traditional dishes. There are several restaurants in the city that provide cuisine from all over the world. Restaurants serving food ranging from Italian and Indian to Middle Eastern and Asian fusion are abundant in the various areas including the Merchant City and Finnieston.

In Glasgow, the traditional British dish of fish and chips is a local favorite. Haddock, which is the most common type of freshly battered fish, is perfectly deep-fried and served with a side of golden fries. Its attractiveness is enhanced by eating it while wandering along the River Clyde or in a busy market.

Glasgow has several delicious dessert options for anyone with a sweet taste. A tasty delicacy is tablet, a crumbly and buttery Scottish pastry made with sugar, condensed milk, and butter. A cup of tea or coffee goes well with pastries, cakes, and scones that are available in the city's bakeries and patisseries.

Glasgow's farm-to-table movement is proof of the city's dedication to sustainability and locally sourced ingredients. Farmers' markets, like the well-known Glasgow Farmers' Market, highlight the best local vegetables, meats, and artisanal goods, allowing customers to taste Scotland's most recent delights.

8.4 Pubs And Bars

Glasgow's thriving bar and pub scene is evidence of the city's strong social fabric, where locals and guests mingle to enjoy companionship, live music, and an extensive selection of libations. Glasgow provides a broad and active drinking culture that reflects its history, inventiveness, and feeling of community, ranging from upscale modern bars to trendy Scottish pubs.

Glasgow's social scene is centered around authentic Scottish bars. These quaint places radiate a warm, inviting ambiance and frequently feature vintage furnishings, dark wood interiors, and crackling fireplaces. Customers are encouraged to relax and interact by the sounds of animated discussions, clinking glasses, and sporadic bursts of laughter that create an authentic atmosphere.

The broad variety of whiskies available in Glasgow bars is a must-do experience. Scotland has a long history of producing whiskey, and Glasgow's bars proudly display this national resource. Scotland also has a great variety of single malts and blends. Customers can enjoy a whisky while conversing about the subtleties of flavor and history that make each spirit special.

Glasgow's pubs not only serve whisky but also a wide selection of regional and foreign beers. The city now has a thriving craft beer sector, with independent and microbreweries fostering an environment that values innovation and originality. Beer aficionados have a wide range of flavors to choose from, including classic ales, potent IPAs, and seasonal beers.

Glasgow's bar scene also highlights its strong ties to the performing and visual arts. Live music performances may be found in many bars and range from modern rock and indie bands to traditional Scottish folk songs. Glasgow's prominence as a cultural hub is highlighted by establishments like King Tut's Wah Wah Hut, which have earned legendary status for helping to begin the careers of well-known performers.

Glasgow's modern pubs and cocktail lounges provide a chic environment for indulging in handcrafted cocktails and creative mixology for those looking for a more modern experience. These chic and fashionable places frequently provide inventive recipes that use regional ingredients to give traditional favorites a distinctive touch.

Pubs, taverns, and late-night establishments can be found in plenty in the West End and Merchant City neighborhoods. These regions invite partygoers to explore a wide range of options nearby with a blend of classic charm and modern flair.

CHAPTER NINE

Day Trips From Glasgow

9.1 Edinburgh

A day excursion from Glasgow to Edinburgh allows visitors to explore Scotland's fascinating history, beautiful architecture, and vibrant culture. These two dynamic towns, which are only a short train trip apart, offer the ideal fusion of historic sites and cutting-edge attractions.

You will begin your day in Glasgow, a city renowned for its Victorian and Art Nouveau buildings. Visit the Kelvingrove Art Gallery and Museum to start your tour; it is home to a diverse collection of works of art and artifacts that span centuries. Explore the picturesque West End, which is teeming with small cafes, boutique stores, and the spectacular architecture of the University of Glasgow.

The stunning Scottish scenery will be visible as you travel to Edinburgh by scenic train. The majestic Edinburgh Castle, built atop Castle Rock, will greet you as you arrive. Discover the castle's ancient chambers, dungeons, and Crown Jewels while taking in the expansive vistas of the city below.

Wander down Edinburgh Castle's Royal Mile, a busy avenue that connects it to Holyrood Palace. Take in the city's medieval ambiance as you are surrounded by historic structures and quaint lanes. Don't skip a visit to St. Giles' Cathedral, a magnificent example of Gothic design, where you can take in the beautiful stone carvings and stained glass windows.

Enjoy a classic Scottish lunch of haggis, neeps and tatties, or fish and chips at a nearby pub. Visit the Palace of Holyroodhouse, which serves as the British monarch's official residence in Scotland, after that. Wander past opulent state residences and take a leisurely stroll through Holyrood Park, which is home to the famous Arthur's Seat, an extinct volcano offering a sweeping view of the city.

Visit the Writer's Museum, which honors the works of Scottish literary greats including Robert Burns, Sir Walter Scott, and Robert Louis Stevenson, to get a flavor of the country's literary past. As dusk falls, go gradually to Calton Hill, another viewpoint with a captivating view of the cityscape, particularly around sunset.

As the day draws to a close, return to Glasgow while thinking back on the historical treasures and cultural marvels you've seen. A day trip from Glasgow to Edinburgh offers an amazing Scottish experience, leaving you with enduring memories of this enthralling adventure. Whether it's the old appeal of Edinburgh Castle, the medieval elegance of the Royal Mile, or the vibrant energy of both towns, they both have something to offer.

9.2 Stirling

A day excursion from Glasgow to Stirling reveals a fascinating tour through Scotland's illustrious past, where historic castles, stunning scenery, and a deep history come together. Stirling offers a nice getaway from the hectic city life and is only a short train journey away.

Your day will begin in Glasgow when you'll board a train headed for Stirling, passing through the beautiful Scottish countryside en route. When you arrive at Stirling, the stirring sight of Stirling Castle, majestically poised atop a volcanic rock, will welcome you. Visit this ancient fortress to start your journey so you can learn about its intriguing history and take in the beautifully maintained architecture.

Take a walk around the bustling Stirling Old Town, which is surrounded by the elegance of the medieval era, in the town's core. Take a stroll around the historic buildings, small shops, and cafes that line the cobblestone streets. Don't pass up the chance to see the Church of the Holy Rude, a masterpiece of the Middle Ages where James VI was crowned.

The National Wallace Monument, a memorial to the fabled Scottish hero William Wallace, is just a short journey away. Reach the top of the monument by ascending its spiral staircase for expansive views of the surrounding area, which include the renowned Stirling Bridge where Wallace won his illustrious battle.

At one of the nearby restaurants, enjoy traditional Scottish fare for lunch while savoring dishes like Cullen skink, a hearty fish soup, or a traditional steak pie. After that, pay a visit to the neighboring Stirling Bridge to fully appreciate the area's natural splendor. This famous crossing was important to Scottish history, and the area around it is a peaceful place to think.

Travel onward to the Battle of Bannockburn Visitor Center, where dynamic exhibits vividly recreate the historic conflict between the Scots and the English. Follow the soldiers' footsteps to learn more about this significant historical moment.

As the day comes to an end, you can stroll about the picturesque Stirling University campus, which is renowned for its gorgeous buildings and verdant landscape. Alternatively, enjoy the peace and natural beauty of the area by taking a leisurely stroll along the River Forth.

You'll have a strong sense of Scotland's heritage when you get back to Glasgow. This day trip from Glasgow to Stirling will be one you'll never forget, full with adventure, discovery, and love for the nation's rich history thanks to the fascinating tales of Stirling Castle, the majestic Wallace Monument, and the battlefields of Bannockburn.

9.3 Loch Ness And The Highlands

An amazing adventure across Scotland's beautiful landscapes, challenging terrain, and renowned natural treasures may be had by taking a day excursion from Glasgow to Loch Ness and the Highlands. After leaving the energetic city of Glasgow, you'll be plunged into a tour of breathtaking beauty and extensive history.

As you go off early in the morning, you'll pass through beautiful towns, gentle hills, and bubbling brooks as you make your way through the picturesque Scottish countryside. The panorama grows more spectacular as you get closer to the beautiful Highlands, with mighty mountains and tranquil glens extending as far as the eye can reach.

Your first visit will be in Loch Ness, a famed freshwater lake famous for its enigmatic depths and the legendary Loch Ness Monster, also known as "Nessie." Enjoy a leisurely sail on the loch's calm waters while taking in the stunning views of the highlands and verdant surroundings. Even if Nessie herself isn't visible, the tranquility of the loch is sure to make a lasting impact.

Make your way to Fort Augustus, a historic settlement perched along the banks of Loch Ness, after your boat tour. You may stroll leisurely along the Caledonian Canal, browse beautiful neighborhood stores, and watch boats pass through a series of locks.

You will pass through Glencoe, an area of astounding natural beauty and historical significance, as you continue your trek into the Highlands. Glencoe's craggy highlands and narrow valleys, which have seen centuries of Scottish history, are breathtaking. Take a moment to pause and capture the breathtaking sights that have mesmerized tourists for ages.

You'll come across the stunning Glenfinnan Viaduct as you travel further into the Highlands, which was memorably shown in the Harry Potter movies. Snap a photo of the famous image as the Jacobite Steam Train passes over the viaduct against a backdrop of imposing mountains and tranquil lochs.

Visit the beautiful town of Pitlochry, which is tucked away in the middle of breathtaking Highland landscape, to round up your day trip before returning to Glasgow. Discover its quaint streets, stop by the neighborhood artisan stores, and perhaps indulge in a dish that is often served in Scotland.

You'll return to Glasgow with a heart full of awe and wonder as the golden rays of the setting sun put a warm glow over the countryside. You will have an unforgettable experience with Scotland's natural beauty and a deep understanding for its rich history and culture thanks to the day excursion to Loch Ness and the Highlands.

9.4 Ayrshire Coast

A day trip from Glasgow to the Ayrshire Coast promises a fun getaway to a location of breathtaking coastline beauty, interesting historical sites, and quaint seaside towns. This lovely beach stretch offers the ideal balance of rest and adventure and is only a short drive away.

You'll begin your day in Glasgow and travel in a lovely car southwest to the Ayrshire Coast. Culzean Castle, a masterpiece of architecture located abruptly on a cliff overlooking the Firth of Clyde, is probably going to be your first destination. Explore the castle's lavish interiors, wander its expansive gardens, and be mesmerized by the mesmerizing sea views from its perches.

You will eventually arrive in the lovely village of Alloway, which is well-known for its connection to Robert Burns, Scotland's national poet. Visit the Robert Burns Birthplace Museum to learn about the poet's life, see his possessions, and take a stroll around the lovely gardens that served as the basis for many of his verses. Don't pass up the opportunity to see the Brig o' Doon, the charming bridge that appears in Robert Burns' well-known ballad "Tam o' Shanter."

You will reach the town of Ayr, a thriving seaside resort with a lengthy maritime heritage, as you go even farther south. Enjoy views of the sandy beach and the Isle of Arran in the distance as you stroll gently down the esplanade. Discover the town's boutiques, eateries, and historic sites, including the Auld Kirk and Ayr Town Hall.

Enjoy some local cuisine for lunch, such as fresh seafood or traditional Scottish dishes, and appreciate the flavors that perfectly represent the seaside area. Continue on your journey to Troon, a quaint fishing resort renowned for its world-class golf courses and picturesque harbors. Take a stroll down the promenade, gaze at the passing boats, and enjoy the laid-back seaside ambiance.

Visit Prestwick, a historic city with deep ties to aviation history, to round out your day excursion. Visit Prestwick Airport, where Elvis Presley first set foot on British soil, and see the Prestwick Golf Club, one of the world's oldest golf courses.

You'll return to Glasgow as the sun starts to set over the Ayrshire Coast, savoring the memories of a day spent among stunning scenery, interesting sites, and the calming rhythm of the sea. A day trip to the Ayrshire Coast provides the ideal fusion of cultural discovery and beach leisure, leaving you with a profound appreciation for Scotland's distinctive and alluring beauty.

CHAPTER TEN

Practical Tips For a Smooth Visit

10.1 Accommodation Options

A variety of lodging alternatives are available in Glasgow, a dynamic city in Scotland, to suit every taste and budget. Glasgow offers guests a pleasant and enjoyable stay with everything from opulent hotels to welcoming bed & breakfasts.

Luxury hotels are a great option for people looking for a little bit of elegance and upmarket amenities. In the center of the city, the renowned Blythswood Square Hotel offers magnificent rooms and suites with rates ranging from £150 to £400 per night. This hotel offers a really opulent experience with its spa amenities, Michelin-starred restaurant, and chic decor.

Options in the middle range strike a mix between affordability and comfort. The Jury's Inn Glasgow is ideally positioned close to popular sites and has rates that range from £70 to £150 per night. Travelers frequently choose it because of its contemporary rooms, on-site restaurant, and ease of access to the city's transportation options.

Budget hotels and hostels are widely available for travelers on a tight budget. With rates ranging from £20 to £60 per night, Euro Hostel Glasgow offers cozy dorm-style lodging. The Z Hotel Glasgow costs between £50 and $100 and has small, tastefully decorated rooms.

Bed and breakfasts have a special appeal that makes for a more personal experience. The Alamo Guest House welcomes guests with genuine hospitality and a homey atmosphere for a nightly rate of between £40 and £100. This choice enables guests to fully experience local culture and savor a handmade breakfast every morning.

Another tempting option for tourists looking for a home away from home is a serviced apartment. With nightly rates ranging from £80 to £150, The Spires Glasgow offers roomy, fully furnished apartments that are great for extended stays or families.

Glasgow has a large number of Airbnb listings, which provide a range of lodging options from individual rooms to complete flats or homes. Prices might range from about £30 to £150 per night depending on the area and amenities.

Glasgow's well-connected public transit infrastructure guarantees simple access to the city's attractions regardless of the lodging option. In order to fully see this vibrant city, travelers can travel efficiently and affordably on the Glasgow Subway, buses, and trains.

10.2 Transportation Options To Glasgow

10.2.1 Air

Glasgow's well-connected international airport and convenient transportation choices make flying there simple and convenient. Glasgow Airport (GLA), which is only 8 miles west of the city center, provides service to the area. This up-to-date, busy airport serves both domestic and international passengers, making it a well-liked entry point for tourists from all over the world.

Glasgow Airport is served by numerous major airlines that offer flights to and from a variety of locations in Europe, North America, and beyond. Both short-haul and long-haul travelers will find it to be a convenient destination thanks to the direct flights that are offered from locations such as London, New York, Amsterdam, and Dubai, among others.

Travelers arriving at Glasgow Airport have a variety of options for getting to the city core and other destinations. The Glasgow Airport Express bus service offers a convenient and affordable alternative, operating around-the-clock and transporting patrons to the city center in around 15 to 25 minutes. For individuals looking for a more tailored and direct transport, taxis and private car hire services are easily accessible outside the terminal.

The Glasgow Airport Rail Link provides a direct connection to the city center for individuals who desire a smooth and timely commute. Paisley Gilmour Street, the airport's railway station, is only a short shuttle bus ride away and offers frequent train service to Glasgow Central Station and other locations in the city. For people who want to travel quickly or with bigger bags, this alternative is very useful.

10.2.2 Train

Train travel to Glasgow is relaxing and beautiful, providing visitors with the chance to take in Scotland's beautiful scenery while efficiently getting them to the city's center. Glasgow is easily reachable from many locations in the UK because of its large rail network.

Glasgow Central Station, which is in the heart of the city, acts as a significant hub for passengers coming from the UK. The station offers a gateway to and from important cities including London, Edinburgh, Manchester, and others and is well-equipped with modern amenities. For those who prefer a more leisurely and ecologically responsible journey, direct train services from London's Euston Station to Glasgow Central can take between 4 and 5 hours.

Scenic routes give passengers a one-of-a-kind and unforgettable experience. One such route is the West Highland Line, which is renowned for its beautiful views of lochs and mountains. Passengers traveling on the West Highland Line get the opportunity to take in Scotland's breathtaking scenery as they travel between Glasgow and the charming communities of Oban and Fort William.

Glasgow's substantial suburban rail network makes it simple for visitors to explore the region outside of the city. It is convenient to reach sights like Loch Lomond and the Trossachs National Park, which offers a wonderful blend of urban and country exploration, thanks to regular and dependable train connections.

Different ticket options, such as advance purchase, off-peak, and flexible pricing, give travelers flexibility and opportunity to save money. Railcards, which provide savings for certain demographics like students, retirees, and families, can also be useful to passengers.

Travelers may easily access the city's public transit system from Glasgow Central Station, including buses and the Glasgow Subway, ensuring seamless connectivity to the city's numerous areas and attractions.

10.2.3 Bus

If you want to see Glasgow and its surroundings, using the bus is an economical and practical alternative. Glasgow is well-served by a vast bus network that links the city to numerous locations within Scotland and even farther away.

Major coach companies National Express and Megabus provide long-distance services to Glasgow from locations in the UK, including London, Manchester, Edinburgh, and more. Bus travel is a desirable choice for tourists on a tight budget because these services frequently offer affordable fares. Compared to a train or flight, the drive allows more time for relaxation, taking in the landscape, and even catching up on work or reading.

The Scottish Citylink bus network connects Glasgow to other significant cities, towns, and attractions, providing a variety of routes for individuals seeking to travel within Scotland or explore adjacent regions. There are many possibilities to fit your plan, whether you wish to see the breathtaking Loch Lomond, the ancient Stirling Castle, or the quaint hamlet of Oban.

Once in Glasgow, local bus services offer a quick and convenient method to get around and discover the city's areas and monuments. Travelers may easily access museums, galleries, shopping centers, and other attractions thanks to the First Glasgow bus company's extensive network that covers the entire city and its surroundings.

The variety of ticket choices available to passengers includes single prices, day passes, and multi-journey tickets. It is now easier for customers to access buses without cash thanks to the usage of contactless payment systems like smartcards and smartphone apps.

10.2.4 Car

Driving to Glasgow is a common option since it provides flexibility and the chance to explore the breathtaking Scottish countryside at your own speed. Travelers may experience both urban and rural views on Scotland's well-maintained road network as they make their way towards the capital.

When you travel by automobile, you can make stops at different attractions and create your own timetable. There are opportunities to discover lovely cities, historical places, and natural wonders en route, making the trip to Glasgow a part of the adventure. For instance, the scenic Loch Lomond and Trossachs National Park is traversed by the A82 route, which offers stunning views of Scotland's fabled lochs and highlands.

The trip from Edinburgh to Glasgow by car takes around an hour and provides a rather direct and short route. Depending on traffic and rest stops, the trip may take 6 to 7 hours if you are traveling from further south, like London. For those traveling from the south, the M74 highway offers a direct route between Glasgow and England.

Glasgow has a ton of parking garages and on-street parking options, so parking is simple to come by. However, it's advised to make plans in advance and look into parking options close to your lodging or travel destinations, especially if you're staying in the city center.

While driving in Glasgow may require negotiating city traffic, having a car gives you the opportunity to visit regions outside of the city limits. If you wish to see outlying sights like the majestic Stirling Castle or the historic New Lanark World Heritage Site, owning a car makes it simple to get there.

10.3 Safety And Emergency Contacts

The majority of the time, Glasgow is a safe city for visitors, but like with any metropolitan setting, it's crucial to be aware of your surroundings and exercise the required caution. Emergency services are easily accessible, and the city has a significant police presence to guarantee the safety and welfare of both citizens and visitors.

Staying in busy, well-lit locations is advised for personal protection, especially at night. Keep your possessions safe and be on the lookout for pickpockets, especially in crowded places and popular tourist areas. Even though there isn't a lot of violent crime, it's still wise to employ common sense and steer clear of conflict.

Glasgow is equipped with a dependable and quick emergency service infrastructure. 999 is the primary emergency contact number for ambulance, fire, and other emergency services. Any phone can be used to call this number, which should be utilized when instant assistance is needed.

By calling 101, you can reach Police Scotland in non-emergency situations. Useful for reporting non-life-threatening occurrences that nonetheless necessitate police intervention, such as minor accidents or theft.

Glasgow also offers a network of healthcare facilities, including hospitals, that offer top-notch medical care. You can visit the closest Accident & Emergency (A&E) department if you experience a medical emergency. There are several different medical conditions that can be treated at the Queen Elizabeth University Hospital and Glasgow Royal Infirmary, two large institutions.

It's a good idea to have a local map or a navigation software on your phone to secure your safety while touring the city, making it simple to get back to your lodging or the closest transportation hub.

You may have a safe and pleasurable trip to Glasgow by being alert, aware of your surroundings, and familiarizing yourself with emergency contact information. Keep in mind that prevention is essential, and that a few basic safety measures can go a long way toward safeguarding your wellbeing while you are visiting the city.

10.4 Local Etiquette

For a successful and happy vacation to Glasgow, it is crucial to comprehend and follow the city's customs. The social interactions and cultural standards of Glaswegians reflect their warm and inviting attitude. Here are some important guidelines for local politeness in Glasgow:

Friendly Discussions: Glaswegians are renowned for their welcoming and outgoing personalities. Asking for directions or chit-chatting with other customers at a pub are both usual and encouraged among the locals. Making small chat and genuinely interested in others is valued and promotes relationships.

Respect and Civility: In Glasgow, respect and civility are highly valued. It is customary to say "please" and "thank you" when speaking with residents, employees, and store owners. Providing a warm smile and holding doors open for others are also regarded as respectful behaviors.

Although Glaswegians are kind, it's still vital to respect personal space and refrain from intruding it. When conversing, keep a comfortable distance and be aware of other people's boundaries.

Glasgow residents frequently queue, notably at tourist sites, transportation hubs, and public locations. Always wait patiently for your turn after joining the end of the line.

Tipping: In pubs, cafes, and restaurants, tips are expected. While not required, giving a gratuity of between 10% to 15% of the total amount is considerate for excellent service. Check the bill because certain places could add a service fee.

Being on time is crucial in Glasgow, particularly for appointments and social events. Being on time demonstrates respect for other people's schedules.

Glasgow has a casual and laid-back dress code, yet it's best to look presentable when going to fancy restaurants or cultural events. For the majority of occasions, casual clothing is appropriate.

Alcohol Consumption: Pub drinking is a popular social pastime in Scotland, a country famous for its whisky. But it's crucial to drink sensibly and refrain from overindulging, especially in public places.

Respect Scotland's historical and cultural legacy by acting with cultural sensitivity. When addressing delicate subjects like politics or religion, be respectful and refrain from generalizing.

Photography: It's polite to get permission before snapping pictures of individuals or private property. Be mindful of any rules regarding photography that may apply to specific locations or attractions.

By adopting these regional habits, you'll not only demonstrate respect for Glasgow's traditions but also enrich your cultural experience and foster relationships with the welcoming residents.

10.5 Sustainable Travel Tips

Glasgow encourages tourists to travel sustainably in an effort to lessen their influence on the environment and enhance their overall experience. Here are some suggestions for eco-friendly travel to keep in mind as you explore the bustling city:

Buses, trains, and the underground are just a few of Glasgow's effective public transportation options. To cut back on carbon emissions and lessen traffic congestion, choose these environmentally friendly means of transportation. The Glasgow Subway, which offers quick access to major attractions, is the third-oldest subterranean metro system in the world.

Cycling and Walking: Take a more environmentally friendly tack by cycling or walking around Glasgow. You may explore the city's neighborhoods and sights at your own pace thanks to the designated bike lanes and pedestrian-friendly paths that are available.

Car Sharing and Rentals: If you need to hire a car, think about going with an electric or hybrid model from a company that values sustainability. Glasgow also offers car-sharing programs that let you rent cars out for a short period of time, thereby lowering the overall number of automobiles on the road.

Stay at Eco-Friendly Accommodations: Pick lodgings that have an emphasis on sustainability principles, such as water conservation, trash reduction, and energy-efficient lighting. Glasgow has a large number of accommodations that are dedicated to green projects.

Local and Seasonal Cuisine: By eating at establishments that use locally produced and seasonally appropriate ingredients, you can support neighborhood businesses and lessen your carbon footprint. Numerous restaurants in Glasgow's thriving food scene place an emphasis on organic and sustainable foods.

Bring a reusable water bottle, shopping bag, and coffee cup to help cut down on the usage of single-use plastics. Many businesses in Glasgow offer water refill stations and support this practice.

Reduce Energy Consumption: Turn off lights, devices, and air conditioning when not in use to conserve energy in your lodgings. Utilizing natural light and unplugging chargers are two ways to reduce your energy usage.

Respect wildlife and the environment by staying on paths and abiding by the Leave No Trace philosophy when exploring parks and natural areas. Don't disturb wildlife, and don't take any plants or flowers.

Respect for local customs and traditions is essential, as is awareness of how your activities affect the surrounding area and the environment. Support authentic experiences that assist locals to practice responsible tourism.

Reduce waste by properly disposing of it and recycling as much as you can. For a cleaner environment, look for recycling containers and abide by the city's waste management regulations.

CHAPTER ELEVEN

Sample Itineraries

11.1 Weekend Getaway In Glasgow

An great weekend escape may be found in Glasgow, a thriving and culturally significant city in Scotland, which mixes historical charm with contemporary attractions and a buzzing environment. Glasgow offers a wonderful getaway with its blend of stunning architecture, top-notch museums, and natural beauty.

Investigate the city's architectural treasures to start your weekend. A must-see is the Glasgow Cathedral, a magnificent specimen of Gothic architecture from the 12th century. Stunning stained glass windows and elaborate embellishments offer a look into the city's medieval heritage. The Necropolis, a unique Victorian cemetery nearby with ornate gravestones and sculptures, makes for an unusual but tranquil visit.

Glasgow's art scene is heaven for art lovers. The Kelvingrove Art Gallery and Museum displays a varied collection, ranging from prehistoric relics to European masterpieces. The Riverside Museum, created by Zaha Hadid, includes a sizable collection of vehicles and provides visitors of all ages with an engaging experience. Architectural creations by Charles Rennie Mackintosh, such as the Glasgow School of Art and The Lighthouse, exhibit his particular style, which had a significant impact on the Art Nouveau movement.

Visit the trendy restaurants, pubs, and shops in the Finnieston neighborhood for a taste of contemporary culture. Enjoy excellent Scottish cuisine while taking in the riverfront scenery. The Barras Market offers a local shopping experience with everything from vintage goods to handmade crafts. It is a busy weekend market.

Glasgow's parks offer tranquility to nature enthusiasts. The peaceful riverbank and rich vegetation of Kelvingrove Park make it the ideal place for picnics and leisurely hikes. You may escape into Scotland's natural splendor by taking a short journey to Loch Lomond and The Trossachs National Park, which provides beautiful scenery, serene lochs, and hiking paths.

Glasgow offers a wide variety of entertainment alternatives throughout the evenings. Attend a performance at the renowned SSE Hydro arena or the Royal Conservatoire of Scotland. Traditional folk music to cutting-edge indie bands can be found in the city's thriving music scene.

11.2 Culture And Arts Exploration

Exploring culture and the arts is a fascinating trip that enables people to become fully immersed in the diversity of human expression, creativity, and history. This complex activity includes a variety of experiences, such as touring museums and galleries, going to live performances, and getting involved with regional customs.

Museums and galleries, which serve as archives of artistic endeavor and human achievement, are at the center of cultural and artistic research. A look into many civilizations can be obtained by visiting museums like the Louvre in Paris, the British Museum in London, and the Metropolitan Museum of Art in New York, which display works of art, antiquities, and historical artefacts that reveal information about the past, present, and even the future.

Another essential component of exploring culture and the arts is live performances. Live music performances, the ballet, opera, and other performing arts venues give artists a stage on which to share their ideas, tales, and feelings. These performances promote a closer connection to the human experience by not only being enjoyable but also by provoking thinking and inspiring introspection.

Local customs and cultural celebrations offer a glimpse into the beliefs and behaviors of a specific civilization or community. Festivals, rituals, and ceremonies provide attendees the chance to see how traditions have been passed down through the centuries, allowing them to appreciate the diversity and individuality of many cultures.

Exploration of culture and the arts must also include practical applications. Participatory workshops, art classes, and interactive displays enable people to express their creativity while learning more about the creative process and developing their own abilities.

Additionally, exploring culture and the arts can greatly enhance one's personal qualities. By exposing people to various viewpoints and lifestyles, it promotes empathy and open-mindedness. As audiences examine and understand the meaning underlying creative creations, it encourages critical thought. Additionally, it promotes a sense of community as people gather to celebrate, debate, and value art and culture.

11.3 Family-Friendly Glasgow

A family-friendly Glasgow itinerary ensures that guests of all ages will have a fun and educational time. Glasgow is the ideal location for a special family vacation because of its assortment of cultural activities, outdoor areas, and interactive venues.

Exploring Culture and History on Day 1 Start your exploration at the Kelvingrove Art Gallery and Museum, which is home to a vast collection of artwork and antiquities that caters to all interests. The varied collection contains anything from well-known pieces of European art to Egyptian mummies. Both children and adults will have an instructive and enjoyable experience thanks to the interactive exhibits and displays.

Go to the busy Merchant City district for lunch. You can find a restaurant or cafe to suit everyone's tastes because of the range of options available.

Take a stroll in George area, the city's primary public area, in the afternoon. While parents take in the historic buildings that surround the square, children can play in the open area and enjoy the fountains.

Day 2: Participatory Adventures Start your day at the interactive Glasgow Science Centre, where youngsters can interact with displays on science, technology, and space. With its informative and visually beautiful movies, the IMAX theater expands the experience.

Visit the Riverside Museum, a transportation and technology museum that will enthrall visitors of all ages, after lunch. Learning about the history of transportation is thrilling thanks to the museum's interactive exhibits and broad collection of vehicles, which includes vintage cars and ancient ships.

Day 3: Nature and outdoor entertainment One of Glasgow's largest parks, Pollok Country Park, offers a chance to reconnect with nature. Visit the Highland cattle, take a leisurely picnic break, and explore the woods trails.

Go to the Glasgow Botanic Gardens in the afternoon. Kids will enjoy exploring the glasshouses, which are filled with bright exhibits and exotic plants. The magnificent Victorian glasshouse known as The Kibble Palace is a highlight that will not soon be forgotten.

Day 4: Activities for the family Visit the Glasgow Tower and the Glasgow Tower Trail, a sister attraction of the Glasgow Science Centre, on your final day. Learn about the city's history and sights while taking in panoramic views of the area.

CHAPTER TWELVE

Resources And References

12.1 Useful Websites And Apps

Glasgow is a thriving city that provides visitors a variety of useful websites and apps to improve their experience. Glasgow is overflowing with culture, history, and a bustling environment. These digital tools can be invaluable travel companions while you take in the city's architectural marvels, delve into its rich history, or hunt for the best gastronomic treats.

Visit Glasgow (Website & App): "Visit Glasgow," the city of Glasgow's official tourism website and app, is a one-stop shop for all things tourism-related. It offers thorough details on sights to see, activities, lodging, food, and transportation. You can easily navigate the city with the help of the interactive map tool.

First Bus App: The First Bus app makes it simple to use Glasgow's public transit system. It's a practical tool for getting around the city effectively because you can get real-time bus timetables, routes, and ticket information.

Historic Glasgow App: The Historic Glasgow app is a gold mine for history buffs. It provides a thorough overview of the city's historic sights, monuments, and landmarks in addition to engrossing tales that vividly depict the past.

The List (website and mobile app): Are you looking for the newest celebrations, events, and cultural activities? The List offers a current overview of Glasgow's entertainment possibilities so you won't miss out on any great events while visiting.

Glasgow Mural Trail (Website & App): Glasgow is known for its thriving street art culture. The Glasgow Mural Trail website and app lead you through the vibrant murals of the city, assisting you in finding undiscovered works of art around every corner.

Yelp (website & app): Yelp's Glasgow section, where you can read reviews and suggestions for restaurants, cafes, and eateries, will appeal to foodies. It's a fantastic tool for learning about regional tastes and culinary experiences.

Hidden Glasgow Forums: The Hidden Glasgow Forums are an excellent resource for learning more about the city's lesser-known features. Engage with other aficionados to learn about off-the-beaten-path sites, forgotten tales, and hidden treasures.

MyGlasgow App: The Glasgow City Council's official app offers up-to-date information on news, events, and city services. It's a useful tool for learning about events and services in your community.

Free Walking Tours: Although they are not digital apps, websites like "Glasgow City Centre Walking Tours" provide information on free guided walking tours that let you learn about the city's history, architecture, and culture from qualified guides.

Google Maps: Without a doubt, no list of practical apps would be complete. You can easily explore Glasgow's streets and neighborhoods thanks to its trustworthy navigation, directions, and real-time traffic reports.

12.2 Recommended Reading

Reading books that embody Glasgow's spirit, history, and distinctive appeal can substantially improve the trip experience for anyone planning to visit the city. The following books, which provide insight into Glasgow's past, present, and cultural tapestry, come highly recommended:

"No Mean City" by H. Kingsley Long and Alexander McArthur: This book provides a vivid and frequently unpolished representation of the streets, people, and struggles of 1930s working-class Glasgow.

Denise Mina's "The Long Drop" digs into the terrifying tale of a serial killer in 1950s Glasgow. The dark underbelly of the city and historical events are expertly woven together in Mina's writing.

From Alan Taylor's edited book "Glasgow: The Autobiography": This anthology offers a fascinating selection of texts from centuries' worth of locals and guests. Readers are given a comprehensive understanding of Glasgow's development through personal narratives, poems, and tales.

Muriel Spark's "The Prime of Miss Jean Brodie" This book captures the spirit of Glasgow and its inhabitants even if it is not specifically about Glasgow. The narrative, which is set in an all-girls school in Edinburgh, reflects the broader cultural dynamics of the era.

John Moore's "Glasgow: Mapping the City" This book examines the evolution of Glasgow's landscape over time, highlighting the growth, urbanization, and architectural changes of the city through the use of old maps and drawings.

"The Dead Hour" by Denise Mina is a compelling crime story that continues the Paddy Meehan series and provides a modern viewpoint on Glasgow's media and criminal milieu.

"Glasgow - A Life in Pictures" by the Glasgow Evening Times: This gorgeous book includes a selection of images from the Glasgow Evening Times archives, highlighting the city's significant events and daily life.

John MacPherson's "Tenement Tales: An Urban Childhood in Glasgow" A memoir that vividly recounts growing up in Glasgow's tenements in the middle of the 20th century, providing a sentimental and touching look into the past of the city.

Gordon Adams' "Glasgow's Grand Central Hotel: Glasgow's Most Loved Hotel" Explore the past of Glasgow's Grand Central Hotel to learn more about its significance to the city's social and cultural fabric.

The Glasgow and West of Scotland College of Domestic Science's "The Glasgow Cookery Book" This classic cookbook provides a look into traditional Scottish dishes and cooking methods for individuals who are interested in culinary history.

These suggested reads offer a variety of viewpoints on Glasgow, from its historical foundations to its contemporary personality. Engaging with these literary works will increase your love for the city and give you a deeper grasp of its inhabitants, culture, and enthralling tales.

12.3 Local Tourism Information Centers

Local tourism information offices in Glasgow are helpful resources for tourists looking for advice, suggestions, and details on the city's attractions, events, and services. These facilities are essential to ensuring that visitors have a seamless and rewarding experience while they are there.

Glasgow iCentre: The Glasgow iCentre is the city's primary tourist information facility, and it is situated on Buchanan Street. The center, which is staffed by experienced and welcoming professionals, provides a plethora of details on lodging, travel alternatives, attractions, and forthcoming events. In addition to buying tickets for excursions and sights, visitors can pick up brochures, maps, and guides.

George Square Tourist Information: Located in the city's center, George Square's information desk gives visitors easy access to crucial information. It's a great place to learn more while seeing the famous square and the nearby buildings.

Buchanan Galleries Visitor Information: Located inside the retail mall, this visitor center serves both locals and visitors. It provides a practical method for obtaining visitor information while perusing the city's retail options.

Glasgow Airport iDesk: For flight travelers, the Glasgow Airport iDesk is a helpful resource upon arrival. The staff can help visitors settle in easily by offering information on lodging, sightseeing, and transportation options.

Riverside Museum: A designated information station at the Riverside Museum offers assistance to both tourists and museum goers. While perusing the fascinating displays devoted to Glasgow's transport history, it's a great place to learn more.

Kelvingrove Art Gallery and Museum: This resource center within the Kelvingrove Art Gallery and Museum provides information to visitors on both the museum's collections and additional local attractions. It's a chance to learn more while taking advantage of the cultural diversity the museum has to offer.

Transport Information Point at Buchanan Bus Station: Providing information on public transportation, routes, and schedules, this information point assists visitors in efficiently navigating the city. It is geared at people coming by bus.

Hotel Concierge Services: There are a lot of hotels in Glasgow that provide concierge services, which include access to travel information and help making reservations for tours, tickets, and events. Personalized recommendations based on guests' preferences can be given by hotel employees.

These regional tourist information offices are priceless assets for travelers, ensuring they have access to reliable and current information to maximize their experience. These facilities provide a memorable and knowledgeable experience in Glasgow's dynamic city, helping with everything from itinerary planning to ticket purchases and insider advice.

12.4 Final Thought

It's tough to avoid thinking about the fascinating variety of experiences Glasgow has to offer as the pages of this travel guide come to a close. The compelling fusion of history, culture, and modernity in Glasgow—often referred to as Scotland's dynamic heart—leaves a lasting impression on everyone who visits.

Glasgow, which is nestled along the banks of the River Clyde, has history ingrained in every aspect of its design. Glasgow Cathedral, a massive Gothic masterpiece, is a reminder of the city's medieval origins. The grand Victorian structures that flank Sauchiehall Street offer an insight into the city's 19th-century industrial development, while strolling through the Merchant City's quaint cobblestone alleyways, one can almost hear the echoes of the past.

However, Glasgow's appeal is not limited by its past. This city has developed into a center for creativity and culture. The renowned Kelvingrove Art Gallery and Museum is home to an astounding collection that includes everything from historic antiquities to cutting-edge works of art. The Glasgow School of Art, a masterpiece of Charles Rennie Mackintosh's architecture, is a testament to the city's impact on the arts.

Glasgow's flourishing live music scene is evidence that music flows through the city's veins. The city reverberates with tunes that capture its multifaceted personality, from little jazz clubs to large concert venues. Not to mention the welcoming pubs and inviting cafés where locals and guests congregate to share tales, laughs, and a pint of Scotland's finest brew.

Glasgow's charm also stems from the friendliness it exudes via its residents. Each visitor is made to feel at home by the friendly and welcoming residents. The bright weekend craft fairs and busy markets like the Barras give you an opportunity to get to know the locals and bring a little bit of Glasgow with you.

The information in this Glasgow travel guide has barely touched on the highlights of this city. Tradition and modernity coexist here, as art and history combine to create a setting that is both energizing and reassuring. Glasgow promises an unforgettable journey that will make you long to go back, whether you are drawn to its rich heritage, its lively cultural scene, or the friendliness of its people. Carry the memories of Glasgow's streets, its residents' joy, and the sense of being a part of something genuinely amazing with you as you go over the world.

Printed in Great Britain
by Amazon

30963681R00066